BOOM TOWN REFLECTIONS

VOLUME – 6

Joshua

By

Mark A. Gregg

An Imprint of Collins Publishing House

4900 California Ave, Bakersfield, CA 93309, USA

Collins's website address: www.collinspublishinghouse.com

First published in English by Collins Publishing House in 2024

1st Edition 2024

Mark A. Gregg © 2024

Mark A. Gregg asserts the moral right

to be identified as the author of this work.

A catalogue record for this book is available

from the Library of Congress United States.

LCCN: 2024924562

E Book ISBN: 978-1-966029-37-3

Paperback ISBN: 978-1-966029-38-0

Printed and bounded in United States of America.

For permission requests, contact info@collinspublishinghouse.com

This book is dedicated to our son, Joshua. You were ours from the very beginning, it just took a while for God's plan to mature and come together. No parent could ever ask for a better son.

Table of Contents

CHAPTER 1
COLUMBIA, MARYLAND

Our time in Garden City, Kansas was now complete. We moved there with the best of intentions in our hearts and then ran from our responsibilities to Delta, Utah before returning in total defeat. The time spent in Delta helped us to re-center, but the return to Garden City proved chaotic and ended dismally as we lost our little Jessica. It was now time for us to leave.

Immediately after losing Jessica, I mailed several resumes to companies that were hiring Shift Supervisor level personnel. One of them went to Engineering Physics Corporation (EP) in Columbia, Maryland. They were not a power plant but a consulting firm specializing in nuclear power plant support services. They also did classified work for the United States Navy and had a small division that dealt strictly with the fossil utility industry. They had an advertisement in Power Magazine saying they had an "immediate need" for fossil plant operators interested in doing consulting work.

I thought it was interesting that they specifically wanted "fossil plant operators" and not nuclear plant operators. I mailed them a resume using my home and work phone numbers, requesting to be discreet if calling the work number.

I heard from them almost immediately. They flew me into BWI (Baltimore Washington International) airport the following week. I had never been to Maryland before, and there was certainly some culture shock.

They lodged me at a beautiful water-front, high-rise hotel located right next to a small, picturesque lake. It was called the

Columbia Inn. I was more than excited about the interview. Engineering Physics' headquarters was located on Hickory Ridge Road in Columbia, about a 30-to-40-minute drive from the airport.

In 1984, Columbia was the most unusual city I ever experienced. It was considered a city of the future. There were no billboards or other advertisements viewable from any road. Businesses were tucked away in tree-shrouded enclaves. The roads meandered intentionally through what looked like countryside when you were surrounded by residential and social settings stealthily hidden in the flora and fauna of the area. The original design of the area was to incorporate many small, welcoming villages throughout the township.

The villages within Columbia had quaint names such as Dorsey's Search, Harper's Choice, King's Contrivance, Long Reach, Owen Brown, and other equally intriguing monikers. Engineering Physics (EP) was appropriately located in a village called Hickory Ridge on Hickory Ridge Road.

Much like everything else in Columbia, the EP office was new, modern, and appropriately adorned for the area. Its location on Hickory Ridge Road was near the end of an ambling, tree-lined drive called Little Patuxent Parkway, which was designed with virtually no straight sections. Everything meandered and curved gently hither and yon through the villages of Columbia.

Unfortunately, no matter how they tried to hide it, everything still moved at a hectic pace in the entire area. It was easy to see why they were trying to emulate nature's blissful serenity. There was certainly little to be found in the picturesque Villages of Columbia.

I arrived early for the interview, wearing a suit and tie. For me, these were Church clothes and frankly, I rarely even wore them to Church. They were, more accurately, my funeral clothes because I generally wouldn't be caught dead wearing a tie and suit jacket. They just didn't fit well, especially the closed collar. It rubbed against my neck and chaffed my skin. I found myself continuously tugging at the neckline of my shirt.

A gentleman named Herman Ashlar met me at the receptionist desk located by the in-house cafeteria/snack bar. I was impressed. They had their own modern restaurant that appeared to have salads, sandwiches, burgers, and the like.

Herman turned out to be a black man. Being from the West, I was around very few black people my entire life. The little burg of Montrose, Colorado where I grew up, never had a black family until I was in high school.

Herman was handsome, soft-spoken, and probably in his mid to late thirties, but I really couldn't tell. He had a solid handshake and genuinely welcomed me to Columbia and EP. He was wearing a nice-looking, chiseled green suit. I thought dress suits were only black or dark blue. Living out west, you don't see many people wearing suits, especially green ones.

Herman looked very dignified. His perfectly round, baby face was oddly smooth and unblemished. There was not a hint of facial hair on him except for his eyebrows. He had the air and persona of a very intelligent, gentleman. I took an instant liking to him.

The interview was low-key, but he asked several technical questions about the plants I worked in. I could tell he knew a lot about the power industry. I viewed it as less of an interview

3

and more of a relaxing conversation about power plants. After he seemed satisfied with our discussion about boilers, turbines, and generators, he introduced me to his boss, Keith Price.

Price was a towering, intimidating, blustery whirlwind of frenetic energy. His massive palm and fingers completely engulfed mine as he vigorously, almost violently, shook my hand. His deep, booming voice and domineering demeanor served to unnerve and rattle me. As near as I could tell, Herman and Keith could not be any more opposite personalities.

I later learned that Keith was a Naval Academy graduate and a former naval officer. Apparently, most of the Engineering Physics management were former Naval officers. Several of the older ones worked for the indomitable Father of the nuclear navy, Hyman G. Rickover. I would later come to thoroughly enjoy the endless anecdotes about this brilliant and driven man's exploits. There are many books available about this giant of a man and his intelligence, drive, and views on war, technology, and life. I personally recommend "The Rickover Effect" by Theodore Rockwell.

My short time with Keith yielded an immediate job offer and pressure to accept it on the spot. I told them I was certain I would accept the position but must talk it over with my wife first. To that, he replied with booming laughter, "Real men make weighty decisions without first talking to their woman." Herman and I laughed also, but deep down, I felt he meant it more seriously than he let on.

The pay and benefits were almost identical to what I had with Sunflower Electric. However, the massive difference in the cost of living between Columbia, Maryland, and Garden City, Kansas, was a formidable and daunting barrier.

Engineering Physics (EP) would pay all moving costs for our household goods and provide us with up to one month's temporary lodging at the Columbia Inn, a very nice high-rise luxury hotel next to the beautiful, ultra-modern Columbia shopping mall. They felt that it would take at least a couple of weeks to find a nice place to live in the Columbia area. Vangie would have to move based on my view and opinion of Columbia, as they would not pay for a house-hunting trip or any means for her to see the area prior to moving.

I was scheduled to return to Garden City very early the next morning, so I called Vangie as soon as I got back to the hotel. She answered on the first ring like she was expecting the call. I bounded into my opening volley.

"They offered me the job on the spot and wanted an answer right then." I paused, reflecting on what happened in Delta, Utah. "I told them I had to discuss it with you and refused to give them an answer."

"Good thing..." There was a pregnant pause. "What's your take on them and the area?" I could tell from her voice she was apprehensive but genuinely curious.

"The area is beautiful. It is green, lush, and ultra-modern. They hide EVERYTHING in the trees. There aren't even billboards. It is like being in the jungle all the time." I paused for effect. "It is certainly 1000 times more scenic than Garden City, Kansas."

"That wouldn't be difficult." She replied drolly. We both laughed. "What about pay and benefits?"

I explained the pay and benefits and told her they would put us in the Columbia Inn for a month, if necessary, while we looked for a place to live. I told her how nice the Columbia Inn was and how there were lakes all around the area.

She grew up boating and water skiing, so I knew this would have a positive effect on her. The icing on the cake was the promise of no more shift work. She knew how badly I hated shift work and how badly I handled it. My inability to properly process shift work also made her life miserable.

The truth is, she wanted out of Garden City as badly as I did. It took very little convincing for her to agree to move there. When I finished talking to Vangie, I called Herman, catching him before he left the office for the day. I accepted the position and told him I would give Sunflower my resignation immediately upon returning to the plant. He seemed pleased and assured me they would have a written offer to me before the end of the week. It was strangely surreal, but we were now leaving Garden City for a second time... *This time, it would be permanent.*

There were no tears from anyone at the Holcomb plant when I resigned. It was the second time I resigned there and would unquestionably be the final time.

Bruce Gorman, an Operator at the Holcomb Plant, heard I resigned and asked if we were selling our house. I told him we were, and he was welcome to come and do a walk-through. He and his wife both loved it and made us an offer we couldn't refuse. Therefore, we sold it quickly and were pleased with the outcome. It put about $3,500.00 in our pocket and relieved us of the burden of selling it while we lived in Maryland.

The long and exhausting road trip to Columbia, Maryland included Brandi and Brittanie trading off riding with Vangie and me. We had two vehicles, which worked well because when the kids got bored, they would irritate each other. Therefore, separating them during the multi-day drive was beneficial to our sanity. After finally arriving in Columbia, we checked into the beautiful Columbia Inn.

The next morning, I checked in with Herman Ashlar and filled out some new employee paperwork before he cut me free to go house hunting. The Columbia Inn wasn't cheap, so it benefitted them by allowing us to find a home as soon as possible. EP provided us with a realtor who specialized in rentals. The realtor drove Vangie, the kids, and me around the different villages as we ventured in and out of too many condos, apartments, and duplexes to even remember.

We were struggling with leaving a 2400 square foot home with a $500.00 a month house payment to viewing apartments and condos that were $750.00 to $1,200.00 a month and half the size of the house we just left. Not a good start, but one that we had to look beyond to assimilate into the fast lane in Columbia, Maryland.

A few days into the search, we found a duplex located at 7223 Sleepsoft Circle. The names of most the roads in Columbia were inventive and even amusing. Near Sleepsoft Circle were streets such as Steamerbell Row, Carved Stone, Better Hours Court, Peace Chimes Court, Harp String, and Minstrel Way. There were virtually no single-family dwellings or *"houses,"* as I liked to call them. If there were "houses" in the traditional sense, we never saw any of them. This was probably because our budget was far, far less than a traditional house would command in price anywhere in the Columbia area.

7223 Sleepsoft Circle became our new home. It was 1200 square feet split between two floors. However, it did have three bedrooms and two bathrooms. Our rent was $800.00 per month, and it was only about a year old, but it was still clean and in perfect shape. We had to get over the fact that we were paying $300.00 more a month for half the space we enjoyed in Garden City. Plus, we had a two-car garage in Garden City. There was no garage nor even reserved parking at the duplex.

The next large item on the to-do list was to find a Church. Columbia was a socialist dreamscape. There was a church building in the village of Owen Brown. It was shared with the Unitarian Universalists and a few other mainline protestant organizations. It seemed to me it was Church for those who wanted a convenient and quick way to say they went to church but with no real commitment. Sharing a building with multiple congregations precludes most of the crucial activities that knit a congregation together as a family.

We found the closest Assembly of God Church was Bethel Assembly of God in Savage, Maryland. Savage was a tiny little burg about 20 minutes from Sleepsoft Circle and about halfway between Baltimore and Washington D.C. Don Cox and his wife, Rose Marie, were the Pastors.

Vangie and I got involved with starting a bus ministry for the church. Our role was limited to helping find and purchase some used school buses and then doing the maintenance needed to get them back on the road. We were reticent to get too deeply entrenched into the structure after what we experienced in Garden City. It's sad how a bad experience robs everyone.

Columbia proved to be a very interesting area to live. We were overwhelmed with the amazing sights within a two-hour radius of our humble Sleepsoft Circle residence. This included the Inner Harbor in Baltimore, the Smithsonian Institute, the United States Capital, and all the monuments in the Washington D.C. area.

In our first months, we tried to get out and see as much as we possibly could. However, a few odd items stand out from our days in Columbia. The first unforgettable sight was driving into inner-city Baltimore and seeing the miles of dilapidated row houses. Even at very young ages, Brandi and Brittanie remember being wide-eyed and unbelieving as we drove through the dense jungle of aging and decrepit row houses.

Seeing the mostly black children playing on the cracked and heaved sidewalks bordering the row houses on one side and tied directly to the busy street on the other side seared an enduring image in our minds. Not only was there not a grassy 'play' area, but the children played just a few feet away from heavy, reckless, stop-and-go traffic framed in the pandemonium of the city that was mere inches from their non-existent 'playground.'

The second unforgettable sight was beholding our first "Toys R Us" store. Coming from modest, western towns, the very thought of having a supermarket of nothing but toys was unimaginable to us. We stopped at our first one outside of Baltimore and took the girls in to see it.

9

We were immediately greeted by people with *SHOPPING CARTS* full of toys. Our mouths fell open, and our eyes bulged as we viewed people filling shopping carts with toys. I was a shallow child, and this proved I was a shallow adult. Why would these two sights be more memorable than, say, the Smithsonian Institute? The Smithsonian is science and history. The streets of Baltimore were reality. *Cold, hard reality.*

With EP, I began what would eventually be a lifetime of frequent travel. I was continually dispatched to different power plants for data gathering and procedural development. Most of my trips were two to three days in duration. I thoroughly enjoyed visiting so many different power plants.

A few years earlier, I had mused that it would be super-cool to have a job where you would constantly get to see different power plants. You know what they say... *"Be careful what you wish for. You may get it."* One of the larger drawbacks was the extensive work involved *after* I saw the plant.

My very first plant visit was the Indian River Power Plant in Millsboro, Delaware. I was wearing a tie and jacket as this was standard attire when doing a sales call. I wasn't a salesman or anything even close, but I was being paraded as one of the technical writers who would be doing their system descriptions and operating procedures.

At the conclusion of the conference room interaction with the Delmarva Power personnel, we took a tour of the facility. It was a large, four-unit plant, and I eventually wrote ALL of their operating procedures.

The plant tour took us down to the large water intake structure located on the banks of the Indian River. While Keith Price and Herman Ashlar were talking to the Plant Manager and other plant personnel, I noticed a dead crab sitting on the ground by one of the large traveling screen units. It was about the size and shape of a football if the air was mostly out.

My attention deficit issues that plagued me for life led me over to the crab. Being from Colorado, I had never seen a crab close-up except in pictures. I decided I would bend over and study this magnificent specimen. With my knees locked and bent completely over at the waist, I put my face about a foot or two from the dead crab.

Turns out it was not even close to being dead. As I bent over, it jumped up, putting its little claws into the air to warn me not to come closer. It scared me so bad that I tumbled backward onto the wet, slimy sand and gravel. I immediately heard my travel companions and the Delmarva personnel bust out laughing.

I was so embarrassed I could barely find the courage to look at any of them. Though he laughed, I saw malice in Keith's eyes as he watched me pick myself up from the ground, trying to wipe the sand from my clothes. Wow! Can I make a great first impression? I could just picture the Delmarva people thinking to themselves, *"This is the moron that will be writing our operating procedures???"*

Vangie, the kids, and I began visiting the Inner Harbor in Baltimore on a regular basis. We enjoyed the excellent restaurants there, and the National Aquarium was a favorite of everyone who visited. Indeed, it was a spectacular and entertaining facility where you could spend hours watching

11

the kids thrill at the sight of multitudes of marine life and the ever-changing aquatic displays.

We settled into a semi-routine existence in Columbia. I was traveling about every other week, so we did not get very involved with Church. Brittanie started Kindergarten there, and one of our favorite family pastimes was walking through the magnificent Columbia Mall. It was, bar-none, the best shopping mall we had ever seen or visited. Café Court in the Columbia Mall was a cacophony of smells, noise, and frenetic movement in and out of the vast number of tables nestled amidst the many eateries.

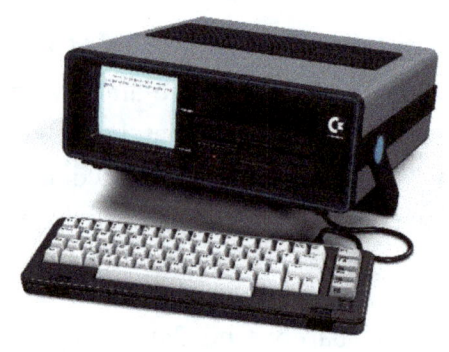

In Columbia, I entered the then seminal and amazing age of personal computers. The original IBM personal computers had been out for about a year and a half, and they were now being 'cloned' and sold at half the price by numerous companies. Unfortunately, even then, we could not afford one due to my previous mismanagement of finances. However, I found an affordable, used Commodore SX-64 *portable* (23-pound) computer. They were first released in late 1983, and I stretched to purchase a good-used one in 1984.

The Commodore's briefcase-shaped 23-pound portable 64 contained all the internal parts of a Commodore 64, including the power supply, 5.25" floppy drive, and a five-inch CRT monitor. *However, it was the first color portable computer ever released.* Though clunky, heavy, and slow, I was able to

12

Commodore SX-64 Circa 1984

write and edit system descriptions and operating procedures *substantially* faster and more efficiently than the other (non-computerized) engineers and technical writers. Up until then, everything we did was hand-written and submitted to the secretaries who would decipher our chicken scratches as best they could while painstakingly entering them into an aging NBI word processor that used undependable and glitch-prone 8.5" floppy disks.

Once they entered and printed our first draft, they would return it for our first edit. We would use a red pen and make it bleed profusely, correcting our mistakes and the many mistakes they made trying to read our barely recognizable handwriting. We would hand it back to them, and they would again decipher our comments, make changes, print it again, and we would go through the same thing for up to five or six iterations. A *terrible* system at best.

Because of this, I also purchased a ridiculously cheap and poor-quality "Gorilla Banana™" dot matrix printer to accompany the Commodore SX-64 computer. I then typed and edited all my documents and then turned them into Herman or the project manager, completely bypassing the secretaries. A few other engineers in the office started doing the same thing with their own recently acquired personal computers.

Our productivity was so much greater than everyone else in the office that a few months later, EP purchased Compaq™ *portable* computers weighing about 30 pounds and sporting two 5.25" floppy disk drives for ALL the technical writers. Productivity skyrocketed despite having to learn the ancient and clumsy DOS™ operating system and complex, equally poor word processing software.

My job in EP was going well. I was moved from a dreary and lifeless cubicle to a coveted and highly desired window office. It was fall, and I could look out at the stunning cornucopia of autumn colors made possible by the grandeur of the Maryland countryside. I was now a part of the 'living' world versus being one of the cubicle zombies in the nether regions. Life was good!

Christmas was the high point of the year for me in EP. I had already been in the window office for a few months when Herman Ashlar came to my office. He seemed far more intense than I had seen him before.

Walking into my office he said, "Mark, you need to go to the fourth floor and see Dr. Deutch, like, right now." He had a look of death on his face and was slowly shaking his head. I was immediately unnerved and freaking-out.

Dr. Deutch owned the company. He was a bit of a legend. His doctorate was in nuclear physics, and he was commonly referred to as a genius. I had never actually seen or met him during my entire time in engineering physics. I could not figure out why he wanted to see me, but I reasoned it could not be good, especially the way Herman was acting.

I entered his large, utilitarian corner office pensively. Numerous diplomas and other memorabilia were prominently displayed on the walls. He was a gaunt, graying, and distinguished man sitting behind an oversized desk. He stood and reached across the desk to shake my hand. "Mark, I am Dr. Deutch, and I am pleased to meet you." He had a firm handshake. I liked that.

"It is very nice to meet you," I replied, looking him in the eyes, trying not to show my obvious and painstaking inferiority, or my intense nervousness.

"I want to thank you for your part in the success of Engineering Physics this year." He reached down and handed me an envelope that was sitting on his desk. My name was typed on the outside of the envelope. I noticed that several other similar envelopes were sitting on his desk.

After handing me the envelope, he continued. "I hope you continue to be part of our team. I have heard good things about you." He paused. "Please, open the envelope."

I opened the envelope and removed a check for $1,000.00. I was stunned. It had 'Christmas Bonus' typed into the bottom.

"Wow! I did not expect this." I was truly caught off-guard by this entire situation. "Thank you, sir, very much. You don't know how much I appreciate it." My sincerity and surprise were genuine and heartfelt.

He just smiled and said, "You have earned this, and I personally wanted you to know how much I appreciate the positive reviews I have received about your performance."

I left his office astonished at meeting him and getting the check. I went straight down to Herman's office. Keith Price and a couple of others were there. As soon as I walked in, they all started laughing!

Herman was the first to speak. "I didn't think you could get any whiter than you are until I told you were supposed to see Dr. Deutch!" They all started laughing again. "You turned so white I think you were glowing!" I laughed with them this time.

I called Vangie immediately after returning to my office and told her what happened. She was as surprised and pleased as I was. We barely lived paycheck to paycheck in Columbia, and Christmas was upon us. This was a badly needed cash infusion for the holidays. I never saw Dr. Deutch again, but I always appreciated him for personally handing me the unexpected bonus check.

All in all, Columbia was a good experience for us even though we missed the West and our families. Unbeknown to us at the time, the most memorable thing about Columbia was about to happen, and it changed our lives forever.

CHAPTER 2
JOSHUA

On New Year's Day, 2005, Vangie, the kids, and I contemplated cooking some burgers on the grill. It was a crisp winter day, but in my opinion, cooking on the grill is not just for summer. There are few things better than a nice, hot, juicy burger in the middle of the winter!

The phone rang as I was looking for charcoal briquettes and lighter fluid. Vangie was squashing out some burger patties, and her hands were covered with burger meat, so she couldn't pick up the phone.

"Mark, answer the phone; it's probably your folks wishing us a happy new year."

I stepped in from the back deck, picked up the phone and cheerfully said, "Happy New Year!" I was expecting to hear family on the other end of the line.

Instead of parents, there was a short pause, and a woman's voice etched with apprehension asked, "Hi... is this Mark Gregg?"

"Yes, it is," I answered, trying to discern who it was.

"Mark, this is Barb Harrison, how are you doing?" We knew Barb and Russ Harrison from the First Assembly of God in Garden City. They moved to Newton, Kansas after Russ received a better job offer. We didn't know them well, but we had been cordial with them during our time together at the First Assembly.

"We're doing really well... How about you guys?" I was making small talk because I could not imagine why Barb Harrison would be calling us. While we knew them, we were not close friends and did not socialize with them when we lived in Garden City other than some Church functions.

"Pretty good, I guess." I could tell by her voice that something was wrong.

"Is Vangie there?" She asked somewhat hesitantly. Before I could answer, she continued. "If you have another phone, have Vangie use it. I really need to talk to both of you together".

I handed Vangie the kitchen phone as she silently mouthed, *"WHAT???"* while raising her soiled hands. I ran upstairs and picked up the extension to be a part of the call. As expected, Vangie was as surprised to hear from Barbara as I was. They quickly exchanged light-hearted greetings before Barb's voice reverted to the heaviness it had earlier in the call.

"I guess I'll get right to the point because I am not sure how to tell you this." She drew a breath before continuing. "A group of us at Church have prayed all weekend for a family that would adopt a little boy whose mom goes to our church here in Newton. The mother is 16 years old and can't give him a decent home. The grandmother is helping raise the child, but she's in poor health and has some serious physical limitations. Anyway, we were praying for a family to adopt the child." She paused for a moment, looking for the right words. "I had a dream last night. It was kind of a special dream that would be hard to explain, but you were the family who adopted this child."

Vangie was obviously as surprised as me. At the time, Brandi and Brittanie were '*it*' for us. Vangie had her tubes tied when Brittanie was born. We were certainly not planning another child.

Vangie was the first to speak. She replied with two carefully measured questions, "what's his name, and how old is he?"

Pat laughed nervously as she said, "this is better than I expected, at least your first words weren't... *FORGET IT*". She paused for a moment. Her voice softened. "His name is Joshua, and he's almost 15 months old".

A shiver ran down both of our spines. The child we lost in Rock Springs was going to be named Joshua had it been a boy. I was quickly swept with emotion. Coincidence? Obviously, it must be a coincidence. Barbara nor very few others knew about Vangie's miscarriage. It happened 7 years earlier and only our closest family knew about it. In fact, Vangie and I had not talked about this in many years.

Vangie was obviously as rocked by this as I was. Our hearts were flooded with thoughts of what could have been and the suddenness of being confronted with this situation after so many years.

We conversed for about thirty more minutes. She explained that Joshua's mother, Carlene, was raised as a church member but rebelled when she was 14 or 15 years old. She took up with a group of kids who were regularly in trouble. She became pregnant, and shortly thereafter, her 18 or 19 year-old boyfriend (the father of the baby) was jailed for armed robbery. He was sentenced to the Kansas State

Penitentiary shortly before Joshua was born and never saw the baby.

Barbara elaborated that Carlene wanted to have the child adopted at birth, but her parents, Robert and Martha, insisted she keep the child. Carlene was still trying to finish High School, be a mother to Josh, and hold down a job while maintaining some semblance of a sixteen-year-old girl's social life. This became too much for her, so she resorted to drugs as an escape. At this point, Martha was almost raising Josh alone which wasn't a good situation at all.

Making things even worse, Martha had a serious heart ailment that precluded physical exertion. This included picking Josh up. He apparently spent most of his time in dirty diapers in a playpen until someone could help her. Barbara told us that about three weeks earlier, the playpen had folded up on Josh, and Martha had to call paramedics to open it up and get him out. She couldn't handle Josh, and he was barely more than a year old. The situation would only worsen with time.

Carlene finally decided that things couldn't continue this way. She wanted Josh to have more from life than she felt she could ever give him. Robert and Martha still wouldn't hear of adoption, so Carlene took the situation into her own hands and went to Barb and Russ for help.

Barb suggested letting a state adoption agency find a home for Josh. Carlene refused because she wanted to know for certain if a good home had been given to her son. She wanted to be part of choosing who raised her child. A state adoption eliminated her from knowing who adopted her baby.

Barb called an attorney to discuss the situation and he assured her an adoption *with no complications* was relatively inexpensive. The biggest expense would probably be a home study the adopting family must complete before placing a child in the home. The lawyer estimated about $500.00 was all the adoption would cost.

Barbara ended the discussion by stating, "It wasn't exactly fair saying you adopted Josh in my dream. You need to decide based on your heart and not outside pressure". Her tone sharpened as she said, "Please seriously consider adopting him, though. I feel very strongly that you guys are supposed to have this child.

It was difficult for Vangie and I to talk about adopting Joshua because of losing Jessica in Garden City several months earlier. We were assured we could adopt that dark-haired, round-eyed, chubby-cheeked, eighteen-month-old cherub only to have her ripped from our arms by a horrendously flawed social services system. Because of this, we were slow to admit we wanted to adopt Joshua. We were also conflicted by his name. *What were the mathematical odds of this situation happening?*

Vangie and I prayed that afternoon for wisdom and guidance. We learned early in our Christian lives that sometimes guidance comes from an open door, not a bolt of lightning or an earthquake, as we would like. The door seemed open, and though we weren't rich, $500.00 didn't seem like too much to gamble for Joshua. After discussing it, we returned Barb's call and told her we were "in."

One of Pat's first questions was a puzzled, "Don't you want to see a picture of him first?"

21

Vangie responded promptly with, "Does what he looks like make any difference?" The subject was immediately dropped, and it was never an issue again.

Tom Astor of Astor and Eppler, the law firm that Barb discussed handling the adoption, called Vangie the next day. She said he seemed very knowledgeable about adoptions and pointedly told her that of all the adoptions he had previously handled, only one child ever reverted to the biological parent. This troubled us because we thought this was a problem only in state adoptions. He repeated what Pat said about the fee being around $500.00, so long as no complications occurred. He said most of the paperwork and research would be done by a legal secretary named Jill, who worked in his office.

When I came home from work that evening, Vangie greeted me at the door. Her usually bright face had an air of tension to it.

"It's decision time." She said slowly as she studied my face for a reaction.

"What do you mean?" I replied cautiously.

"If we really want to adopt Joshua, we must pay all fees out front, or else the lawyer won't handle the adoption." I set my briefcase on the chair and loosened my tie.

"Is there any question in your mind?" I asked, knowing what her answer would be.

"No, at least not to the adoption, but do you think we can afford it right now?"

"Probably not." I musingly replied. "But it's never stopped us from doing things before."

While our move to Maryland from Kansas was well covered financially by EP, we weren't prepared for the much higher overall cost of living in Maryland. We were paying a $500.00 dollars a month house payment for our large, roomy home in Kansas. When we moved to Maryland, we had to pay an $800.00 monthly rent payment for our small duplex.

We stacked the basement to the ceiling just to get all our household and garage goods to fit. With no savings, all we had left was credit. Our Visa card was good for $3000. We didn't use it much because I figured that without savings, it was our emergency backup that savings normally would be. I made a $500.00 cash draw against the Visa card and sent it to Tom Astor the next day.

"All that's left now is waiting," I told Vangie at the evening dinner table. *Unfortunately, I couldn't fathom just how far wrong I was.*

CHAPTER 3
ROADBLOCK AFTER ROADBLOCK

Life was quiet for the next couple of weeks. Barb called about every other day to see if we heard anything. Each time, Vangie assured her she would call if we did. We assumed everything was going well until Jill, the Legal Assistant, called us one day with some bad news.

"Maryland won't allow private, interstate adoptions." She seemed truly concerned and apologetic as she was giving me the bad news.

"What can we do?" I asked, knowing there had to be some way to handle the problem.

"This is a bigger problem than I can handle," she said frankly. "You'll have to talk to Tom." I knew every time Tom Astor was brought into the case, it was an expense above and beyond the original quote.

She connected me to Tom. He explained that all interstate adoptions were coordinated through each state's *Interstate Compact Commissioner.* He said the Commissioners were basically free to do what they liked, even to the extent of allowing interstate adoptions.

Maryland's Interstate Compact Commissioner was a man named Bud Nogle. Tom said he would personally call him and try to get this straightened out. The more he spoke, the more cash flowed freely out of my wallet.

Wednesday of the next week, the situation began deteriorating even further. Tom called that morning and told us Bud Nogle was a very "abrupt and abrasive man" who wouldn't even consider allowing the adoption. Our only option was to establish a residence in Kansas until after the adoption and then "move" back to Maryland.

We were crushed but not defeated. We called the Reveres back in Garden City and asked them to find a cheap furnished apartment for rent and call us back. We made it clear that we needed an address and that the "apartment" could be a dump just so it was cheap.

Thinking we handled things well, we sat partially at ease until later that afternoon when Barbara called and was extremely upset.

"Martha kidnapped Joshua," Barbara said almost hysterically. "She just found out that Carlene was trying to have Joshua adopted, so she took him and left."

Things seemed in a tailspin now. Martha's health was bad, and she had Joshua in a car going to who knows where. Barbara explained that Bob, Martha's estranged husband (Carlene's dad), lived in Emporia. Barbara knew they were on speaking terms and thought she might be going there.

We felt helpless as events unfolded back in Kansas that we had no control over. We later learned it was probably a good thing we weren't there. The Lord had a plan and always made a difference, no matter the situation.

You could cut the tension in our household with a knife for the next few days. Vangie and I stayed out of each other's way to avoid discussing the situation. It was the best thing we could do because we knew anything we discussed wouldn't change things anyway. I know that during this time, we spent a lot of time praying. Neither one of us felt the Lord was closing the door to this adoption. We were just annoyed at how complex things had become.

Barbara called two days later. She sounded relieved, though her voice courted much tension when she told us the good news.

"I've got Josh." She said in a measured, careful manner. "Martha went to Emporia for a day apparently to scare Carlene into not putting Josh up for adoption. When she returned, she made Carlene promise not to do anything stupid. As soon as Carlene got the chance, she grabbed Josh and brought him over to us."

"What are you going to do now?" Vangie asked, shaking her head at how complicated this 'simple' adoption had become.

"I guess Russ and I will keep him until the adoption is final." Her tone softened. "He's a really good kid. We won't have a problem getting along".

"What about Carlene? Where's she going to stay?" I could tell by Vangie's voice that she was upset over how complex this entire situation had become.

Barbara apparently sensed it also. The tension in her voice relaxed as she said, "Don't worry about a thing, we're fine, Josh is fine, and Carlene is fine. Besides, it will give us a chance to keep an eye on Carlene." She stammered as if she didn't want to complete the sentence. "In case she starts to break."

We talked long enough for me to realize the tremendous pressure on Carlene. She was having a problem holding a job, her mother was putting an incredible guilt trip on her, and to top it all off, her dad was, as Barbara put it, "a wild man."

Barbara was concerned that Carlene was relying on drugs to help her cope each day. She said that when Carlene brought Joshua over, she seemed "out of it." This concerned me a great deal. I tried to imagine what it was like being a young girl in her situation with no place to go and with everyone you love seemingly against you. I went upstairs, wept, and prayed for Carlene's strength. She was going to need it.

Tom Astor again attempted to persuade Bud Nogle to allow the adoption. This time, however, he did it in writing. Not only did he receive no response by mail, but when he called Bud's office, the secretary told him that Bud "discarded the letter because it was a waste of time to pursue it any further... Maryland does NOT allow private interstate adoptions!"

When Tom called to tell us this, he had more bad news. He sounded very concerned as he stated, "Mark, no one alive could foresee the problems that have occurred. I was looking at your time tickets that Jill keeps, and I see that we have already spent the $500.00 you sent. Before we go any further, you will need to send us some more money."

I was steamed! I didn't particularly feel I received my money's worth on the first $500.00, and now he was asking for more. He explained that Jill did a lot of necessary paperwork with the State of Kansas and that the remainder of the money was spent trying to convince Bud Nogle to accept the adoption in Maryland. He convinced me that we could get around Bud and that the adoption was still a reality. (All it takes is money).

I did another cash draw on Visa and sent Tom $500.00 dollars more. I then did something that shocked even me. I called Bud Nogle's office to confront him personally. I think I was so frustrated over not being able to help with the problems in Kansas that I decided to involve myself in things here.

It took numerous tries to get past Bud's secretary. When I did, I was plenty surprised at what I got.

"Bud Nogle speaking." He had a terse and impatient manner.

"Uh, yes, Mr. Nogle," I began in my best business oratory. "My name is Mark Gregg, and my attorney in Kansas has tried to talk to you about an interstate adoption with no success."

"Doesn't surprise me." Bud interrupted rudely. "I don't deal with private adoption lawyers." I was stunned for a moment. I didn't expect this response from a man in his position. I regained my composure and continued.

"My wife and I moved to Maryland about 5 months ago. We presently have two children, both our own, and we would like to adopt a child that is presently in Kansas."

"Are you adopting from a relative?" he asked almost rhetorically without thought.

"No, she is a sixteen-year-old confused kid who is under a lot of pressure."

"Tell that confused kid to turn the child over to the state of Kansas, and I'll be happy to allow an interstate adoption." I could feel my temper rising, but I knew I had to keep my cool.

"Sir, I think she would, but out of love for the child, she wanted a hand in picking the adoptive parents."

"How much are you paying her for the child?" His voice turned *openly* cynical.

"I can barely afford to pay the lawyer $500.00, let alone pay the mother anything." There was a long pause. A shiver went up my back as I waited for him to make the next move.

"Get a home study done from one of the private social service organizations. I can't promise anything, but if the home study looks okay, I may consider the adoption."

I couldn't believe my ears. I guess I didn't expect to get anywhere with him. I called Vangie after talking to Bud. Hearing some positive news really picked up her spirit. I left her in charge of calling some of the various social service organizations in the Baltimore area to request a home study.

Any joy I perceived in Vangie when I called earlier was gone when I came home from work. The minute I walked in and saw her face, I knew she hit a snag.

"What's wrong now?" I asked hesitantly.

"I only found one social service organization that would even attempt a home study in the next year." She became almost belligerent as she spoke. "They want between $1500.00 and $2000.00 and told me it will be five to six months before they can even get around to it."

"We'll just have to use the card," I announced after a pause to consider the situation. "We'll pray that Tom Astor's bill won't be any more than what we've already sent him."

Vangie called and ordered a home study the next day. Agreeing to an extra $300.00, they put an "expedite" on our case to hurry things up. She also called the Finney County Department of Social Services back in Garden City. They did their own home study on us when we became foster parents for Jessica. It was barely a visit to the house and an hour of discussion with us about Jessica and the expectations of being foster parents. Nothing that would qualify as a home study for an adoption. However, they generously agreed to send us the little information they had taken. They felt it might possibly reduce the price of the home study we were getting in Maryland.

Later that same day, Denay Helms from the social services office in Garden City called Vangie. Denay was the case worker handling Jessica's case when we were her foster parents. She was a very dedicated lady who secretly detested the laws that put children back into unfit homes. She even cried with us the day the judge ruled in favor of Jesscias's mom and ordered her placement back in the home.

Denay told Vangie she overheard the records clerk tell someone she was sending a copy of our file to us. After finding out why, she called us.

"We generally exchange favors with other states when a home study is needed in state-handled adoptions," she explained confidently. "Officially, we aren't supposed to do it, but it happens all the time. The problem in your case is that it's a private adoption." She stopped in an apparent effort to choose her next words carefully. "What I can do is call my counterpart in Maryland. If he or she isn't too busy, I might be able to talk her into doing a state-sponsored home study. It may not work, but it's worth a try anyway." Vangie and I couldn't thank Denay enough. We prayed her plan would work even though it was a long shot.

Things were quiet again for a few weeks. Unfortunately, it was the calm before the storm. Barbara called one Sunday night as we were finishing our dinner. She was crying.

"Things are bad here," She sobbed. "Martha reported Carlene for drug abuse and is filing charges claiming she is an unfit mother."

Her anguish was painfully evident as her sobs grew louder. "She and Bob, Carlene's Dad, came to the house about an hour ago because they heard we had Joshua. Russ slipped out the back door with Joshua while I talked to them at the front door. Bob went crazy and started screaming obscenities at me and threatened to kill me and burn us out. When I shut and locked the door, he called me names through the windows that were beyond belief. The man's crazy. I was scared to death he was going to break a window and come in and kill me. Our kids were terrified and crying, and I didn't know where Russ had gone. I called the police because I was so scared... I just didn't know what else to do."

"Just calm down and try and relax," Vangie said soothingly. Barbara didn't normally seem to be an emotional person. It was obvious she was truly scared. She went on to tell us that Carlene had "disappeared" two days earlier. The tension was apparently too much for her and she had just dropped out of sight.

We asked Barbara if she could try to find her. We were hoping she could help her get her head screwed on straight. If she didn't, everything to date was wasted. Barbara said she thought she knew where she went and would get in touch with her if she could.

31

We were finally having our first real doubts about the adoption. We prayed long and hard that night for direction. Unfortunately, the next day brought more bad news. Tom Astor called and said the only way the adoption would ever "stick" was for Carlene to have a complete physical examination, including drug tests. If she made it through that okay, she needed a psychological exam done by a qualified Doctor to determine she knew exactly what she was doing. Then, and only then, would he bring her before a judge to sign the adoption papers.

The bottom line was money. Each one of these things was in addition to the money already spent. He needed a check for at least $1500.00 more to even continue. I felt we had no choice and did another cash draw.

We called Barbara that night to tell her about Tom's call and what he required of Carlene. Turns out Carlene was there. It was odd to suddenly be faced with talking to her. Up until now she had been a troubled teenage girl for whom I had much compassion. Now, she was a real person and I knew I would have to choose the right words when I talked to her. I said a small prayer under my breath. Barbara asked if I would like to talk to her. I pensively agreed.

Barb passed the phone to Carlene. She spoke slowly and timidly. "Hi, this is Carlene. Barbara said you wanted to talk to me?" Her voice was more mature than I anticipated. I wasn't exactly sure what to say to her, and I'm sure she felt the same way about me.

"Carlene, hang in there." I could feel myself grasping for words. "I know things don't look particularly good right now, but everything will work out. I'm more concerned about you than the adoption. Are you going to get through this, okay?" I could tell she was trying not to cry as she spoke.

"I'm okay. I just feel so bad about everything that's happened and how much money this must be costing you."

"Don't worry about that stuff. You just worry about keeping yourself together."

Her voice seemed to relax as she said, "Barbara has told me a lot about you and Vangie. She hasn't told me your last name or told me where you live... But it's probably for the best that I don't know. I just want you to know that I truly love Joshua. If I didn't love him, I wouldn't be doing this. I can't give him anything in life right now." She began openly crying. "I don't care what anybody says. It would be far easier for me to keep him than to give him up. Please, please realize that."

A lump formed in my throat as hot, salty tears rolled down and stung my cheeks.

"I fully realize that," I said, trying not to let my emotions show. "I think you are doing something... Something very brave. Very few mothers would do what they are doing because they bend to the pressure of others instead of doing what is right. Please understand that we know what pressure must be on you right now. If there is anything we can do to reduce the strain, we'll do it. As far as the adoption, money, or anything else, please don't worry about it. I've seen enough happen now to know the Lord's hand is in this, so I don't believe it can fail."

"Let me tell you a little story." I began slowly as she remained silent. "When Barbara called us New Year's Day and told us about a little boy named Josh and that she had a dream we adopted him, I knew in my heart that this whole thing was of the Lord." I paused to steady my quivering voice. "About seven years ago, our oldest daughter was a year old when Vangie got pregnant again. We weren't very excited at first, but as time passed, we felt much better about it. We had almost convinced ourselves the baby was a little boy and that we would name him Joshua David." She began sobbing as I spoke. "Then, one night, without warning, Vangie got really sick. I took her to the hospital, but it was too late. She lost the baby. The doctors never gave us an explanation of what happened. I don't think they knew, but I know now that we are supposed to raise this child."

"I really needed to hear that." She said between sobs. "I'm so confused because of everything my parents are saying, but somehow I know that I'm doing the right thing." We talked for a few minutes more. I told her about the physical and psychological exam she must take. She assured me she would be ready and would pass both. It was difficult to say goodbye to her. I knew she was hurting badly and needed all the comfort and reassurance she could get.

Tom Astor called about a week later to tell us he scheduled Carlene for her examinations. He explained that if she wasn't 100% drug-free, he would drop the case because it probably wouldn't go through anyway.

The expense for both exams and his services to bring her before the judge to sign the adoption papers was high. He needed $500.00 more dollars. I made a final cash advance. I was getting worried now. If we didn't get the "free" home study done by the state or if there were many more problems, the financial cistern would be dry. This $500.00 adoption was driving us to the poor house.

Another week went by. We were becoming uneasy because we hadn't heard anything about the home study. However, it didn't matter. We received the worst news on Wednesday. When Joshua was born, Carlene declared Jimmy Dean Hoffman as the father of the child rather than declaring him unknown. Tom was apologetic that it hadn't been caught sooner.

"Jill should have caught this earlier." Tom angrily stated. "It may not be a problem, though, he'll just have to sign parental rights away."

"What's that going to entail?" I asked, afraid of what I was going to hear.

"Well... I'm not entirely sure." He replied uneasily. "If he doesn't want to sign the papers, we'll have to file suit against him for abandonment. That could take months and would cost a great deal of money. Depending on his defense, I don't think we could win anyway."

"Great," I replied in total disgust. "How soon will we know anything?"

"I've got Jill working on it right now. She's going to the penitentiary with the papers to see if she can quietly get them signed. Just as soon as I hear anything, I'll call." We didn't have long to wait for a reply. Tom called us back about an hour later with more bad news.

"Apparently, Carlene's mom went to Jimmy's folks and convinced them something was rotten about this whole thing. Mrs. Hoffman called right after I talked to you and said she advised Jimmy not to sign anything."

My heart sank. I couldn't believe this was happening. I was so sure the Lord had ordained this adoption, and now it seemed impossible.

"What now?" I grimly asked.

"Well," he began slowly. "Jimmy's folks have lived here for many years. Jimmy and his brothers were adopted." He paused as if to re-evaluate the situation. "I believe that is on our side. They've been through what you are going through three times already... I'm sure they know how it feels to be in your shoes. Besides, all three of their boys are presently in some type of trouble. I somehow don't think they want to endure anything else if they can help it."

"Then why did they stop him from signing the papers?" I demanded.

"I don't really know. It could have been something Martha said, or they may need assurance this whole thing is on the level. I casually know Jim Hoffman. I am told he's out of town right now, but when he returns, I'll make an appointment to talk to him personally."

Vangie and I were both depressed. Everything seemed to be going in the wrong direction. I knew everything Tom was doing was costing more money. We hadn't even heard from Maryland Social Services yet. If the "free" home study fell through, we would be sunk. There just wasn't more money to spend, and right now, it looked as if it were futile to spend it anyway.

Once again, everything slipped into an ominous silence. The days slipped by with a grinding tedium. Our lives seemed in a relentless hold pattern. We were suspended like helpless marionettes dangling from the clutches of people we had never met and who seemed to not care about Joshua. We didn't talk about it much, mainly because there was nothing new to say.

Joshua was a continuous topic of Vangie's and my prayers. I reached the point where I didn't know exactly what to pray anymore. The Lord and I discussed it so much that it was almost routine to pray for strength for Carlene and to help us through whatever the latest crisis was taking place.

I'm convinced many of the "battles" already won in this adoption process were done so through the spiritual realm by faith in Christ. In Ephesians 6-12, the Apostle Paul stated that our battle is not against flesh and blood but against powers and principalities of wickedness in high places. It's interesting to me that many Christians know and at least casually accept this, and every non-Christian doesn't know it or laughs at it if they do. I think very few of us, Christian or not, take this seriously enough. We should do this because if a battle to further the kingdom of God is going to be won, in every case, it will be won in the spiritual realm through Christ Jesus *first.*

We talked to Barbara every few days. It was obvious keeping Joshua was creating a strain. Not so much because she didn't want to keep Josh but because of the tensions with Carlene's parents and tensions at church. Since they attended the same church, it was obvious to all what was happening. This caused people to quietly take sides, a very human reaction even though they should have stayed out of it. Barb and Russ quit attending church during this time to prevent any potential problems from occurring.

A few weeks later, Carlene finally took her "fitness" tests. We never received official results, but the word from Barbara and Tom Astor was good. In fact, they said she passed everything with "flying colors." This included signing the adoption papers in front of a very obnoxious and persistent Judge who determined "beyond a shadow of a doubt" that Carlene fully understood what she was doing.

We were obviously pleased by all of this except for the hurt Carlene suffered when she was degraded and chastised by the judge while he was assuring himself that she was fully cognizant of her actions. We were desperately looking for some good news. It was about to arrive in a Divine moment that is etched forever in our memories.

CHAPTER 4

UNQUESTIONABLE DIVINE PROVISION

The day after Carlene signed the adoption papers, Tom called. He told us that Carlene passed her tests and signed the papers. He also had some news that wasn't so good. He was at an impasse with the Hoffman's and $1082.00 in arrears in our account.

He explained that if the Hoffmans changed their minds tomorrow, he would still need the money presently owed him before going any further. Payment of the $1082.00 would cover everything to date, plus finish out the adoption if the Hoffmans changed their minds. He apologized for letting the account get in arrears. Apparently, Jill was tied up on another project and was not tracking ours as closely as she should have been. The costs added up quickly because of the drug tests and Doctor fees.

That night, Vangie and I were wearing our feelings on our sleeves. We picked at each other over little things while avoiding a discussion we knew was inevitable. We were out of money and didn't know if we could get Josh now or not. We decided to pray together before we went to bed that night. We didn't pray together often.

We asked the Lord for confirmation that we were acting in his will. We could probably get a loan for the money, but the way things appeared now, it still wouldn't get Joshua to us. It was difficult to pray, but we pushed through.

We had, once again, reached the point where we were questioning if we had been wrong all along. Was the adoption really of the Lord, or was it just something we wanted? We weren't looking for a child when Josh came along, so maybe we just got caught up in the spirit of the thing. This would explain why it hadn't gone smoothly. Surely, if the Lord truly wanted us to have Joshua, *He would have made a way.* We finished praying by asking one more time for confirmation that it was His will.

I went to Delaware for the next two days to work at the Indian River powerplant. I couldn't call Vangie that afternoon as I usually did when I was at my office, so I called her when I got to the hotel that night. She picked up the phone after the first ring.

"Hello?" I could tell by the way she answered that something had happened. There was an urgency in her voice, and Vangie is rarely excitable.

"Hi honey, how was your day?" I asked pensively.

"Mark, you are not going to believe this." She seemed very excited, and she was talking as if she, herself, didn't believe what was to follow.

"What? Is something wrong?" It alarmed me to hear this much emotion in her voice.

"We received two checks in the mail today. They total $1090.00."

"From who?" I could hardly believe it was true.

"One was from Valley Savings and Loan for $948.00. The other was from the State of Utah, for $142.00."

I went momentarily numb. It was like I stood up from a rest too quickly and was disoriented. "Are there any explanations for the checks?" I asked, still not believing any of this to be real.

"The State of Utah check has OVERPAYMENT OF 1983 STATE INCOME TAX printed on it. The Valley Savings and Loan check has a letter in it that says they've had a problem on their books for almost two years and finally traced it to the house we sold on Arapahoe Street in Garden City". She paused as if to question the whole thing. "They say we overpaid them at the closing, and no one caught it until now."

It was obvious we had just experienced the power of God! *The Lord provided for Joshua's adoption before he was even born!* As soon as I got off the phone, I fell to my knees and began thanking the Lord. I honestly don't know how long I cried and worshipped that night. My eyes were swollen the next morning as I looked in the mirror to shave.

What happened was not fulfillment of a material need, though it did do this, but it was complete divine confirmation of what we were supposed to do. He provided what we needed at the very moment we needed it. In fact, He obviously knew about the adoption long before Joshua was even born because these checks were prompted by actions that happened over *two years earlier!*

The Lord responded in a supernatural way to our request for direction and guidance. I now knew that I would fight for my son with everything Holy and necessary to bring him to us.

The next Monday, Tom Astor called. I could feel his excitement as he spoke. "Mark," he began quickly, "I don't have the slightest idea of why he changed his mind, but Jimmy Hoffman decided the best thing to do was sign the adoption papers. He feels Joshua would be better off in an adoptive home than with Carlene, and he knows he obviously can't raise him." He hesitated and slowed his pace. "This was the first time I've actually talked to him. He seems to be a pretty sharp kid. It's too bad he ended up where he is. Anyway, Jill is taking the papers to him tomorrow.

"You mean this is it?" I asked unbelievingly.

"It would be if the State of Maryland were satisfied, but I'm afraid that may be a serious problem for you. Since you have talked to Bud Nogle and had better luck with him than I did, I would suggest you speak with him again and find out where you stand. We'll send the adoption papers to his counterpart here in Kansas. She can forward them on to Bud." He paused as if to smile. ***"Congratulations, it's a boy."***

When Tom and I finished, Jill came on the line to ask what we wanted to name our new child. It was necessary to get the new birth certificate printed. I told her I wanted to name him after a child we lost several years earlier; *"Joshua David."*

Vangie was very excited that night. We called and told Barb the good news, but we found out that, again, things were not going quite so well in Kansas. Carlene had disappeared a second time, and Martha and Bob were making her and Russ "prisoners in their own home." They had kept Joshua for several weeks now, and it was becoming almost an unbearable strain. I knew we had to do something quickly for everyone's sake.

Vangie and I prayed together that evening after talking to Barbara. We asked for help through what appeared to be the final milestone in Joshua's adoption... *Bud Nogle and the State of Maryland.* We had already made up our mind to re-establish residence in Kansas if Maryland became too large of an obstacle. However, this was going to be a financial problem. I knew I must speak to Bud Nogle again.

As before, it took numerous tries to reach Bud at his office. When I finally reached him I was greeted in the same chilly, abrupt manner as before.

"Mr. Nogle?" I began cautiously. "This is Mark Gregg. I spoke to you several weeks earlier about bringing an adopted child into this state."

"So?" He impatiently replied after several moments of silence. It was almost embarrassing.

"Well, if you recall, you told me I could bring the child in-state if we completed a home study."

He grunted before almost flippantly replying. "I talk to a lot of people and can't recall the details of the many conversations, but please continue."

"All of the adoption papers are signed, but we haven't been able to complete the home study. Is there any problem bringing the child into the state temporarily until the home study is completed?"

"What state is handling the adoption?" He asked. He had an air of perpetual impatience, almost arrogance, about him.

"Kansas is the state he's coming from," I cautiously replied. "However, it's a private adoption."

"We don't allow private interstate adoptions." His tone switched from impatient to angry.

I immediately snapped. In my mind, I envisioned Jessica and how she was needlessly placed back in a destructive

43

environment by people as ignorant and self-centered as this man. I boiled further as I thought of everything we had already endured in this adoption. And now, one man was again jeopardizing everything.

"Sir, we've been through this already." My voice grew steadily louder. "You personally okayed the adoption pending completion of a home study. I don't know what your problem is, but there is a fourteen-month-old boy who has been booted around needlessly far too long already. It's all because the system doesn't protect the kids it's supposedly designed to protect but instead protects the bureaucrats paid to do a job. The saddest thing of all, is if I had any money, you would be powerless to stop the adoption anyway. However, because I'm barely a middle-class person trying to use the system as it was designed, I'm penalized... Excuse me, in this case, the adoptive child is penalized because I was foolish enough to follow the rules."

I rarely raise my voice to people. The reason is the sick feeling I get in my stomach after realizing that all chances for progress are probably destroyed. I decided that I must bail myself out.

"Sir, I honestly apologize. Please forgive me. I don't usually talk this way. This whole adoption process has weighed heavily on us, and I have no right taking it out on you." There was a silence that seemed like hours but was probably just a few seconds.

"What's the problem with the home study?" He sounded almost human now.

"The State of Kansas sent you all of our records from when we were foster parents. We were hoping this would

44

reduce the cost of a home study here. The problem is, we've never heard whether Maryland has even received the papers... It's been several weeks."

"I'm going to put you on hold for a moment. If the State of Kansas sent anything, it's probably here in this mess." His candor surprised me. Several minutes later, he picked the phone back up.

"Mr. Gregg, has the State of Kansas sent the adoption papers to us?"

"I believe they're in transit right now."

"That's why I couldn't find them..." His voice trailed off. I could hear papers shuffling in the background. "What is the child's name that you're adopting?"

"Joshua Curtiss," I replied, wondering where the conversation was headed now.

"I've got your foster parent file from Kansas here in front of me. It apparently came to me some time back." His voice turned defensive. "I filed it because there was no explanation attached to it, and I didn't have any idea what I was supposed to do with it." He paused to shuffle some more papers.

"As far as I'm concerned, you can bring the child into the State when I get the signed adoption papers from Kansas."

I was completely stunned and not entirely sure we were communicating on the same level so I questioned his direction. "How much time will we have to get a home study done after he arrives?"

"As far as I'm concerned." He began authoritatively, "What I have here is sufficient. All I need is the adoption papers on file, and the child is yours."

Once again, I knew we had experienced the power of God. I called Vangie and gave her the news. She was as stunned as I had been.

"When can I go get him?" She asked excitedly.

"Probably any day now. Tom said he would send all the adoption papers to the State of Kansas, and they would forward them to Maryland."

It took about a week for Bud Nogle to get all the papers. They arrived about four days *after* Joshua David arrived at his new home. Things were deteriorating enough in Kansas that Vangie flew and picked Joshua up. Barb and Russ took him from Newton to a hotel near the Kansas City airport where Vangie stayed after her arrival. She immediately returned to Columbia with our new little boy named Joshua David.

Let's review all of this for a moment...

The child's birth name was the same name we chose for the child we lost several years earlier.

Divine Providence set aside the money for the final adoption payment before Josh was even born. Both of the completely unrelated checks arrived the same day and for virtually the exact amount owed to finish the adoption. One was from the State Government in Utah, and the other was from a bank in Kansas. Both of the unrelated errors that led to the payments were discovered and paid at the same time.

The simple 2-hour home study completed in Kansas for the foster parent program sufficed for the adoption home study in a state that demanded an extensive home study to adopt a child. A home study that normally costs thousands of dollars.

I think the facts speak for themselves. And yet, some people will read this and pass it off as *coincidence, lies, or bluster.* Sad.

CHAPTER 5
THE FINAL DAYS IN COLUMBIA

We fell into somewhat of a rut while living in Columbia. I was continuously on the road working at several different power plants. This wasn't ideal for home life, especially with three small children. I usually arrived home exhausted and just wanted to kick back and relax. However, Vangie made it *abundantly* clear that the kids needed quality time with Daddy, and she could use the break.

Vangie was absolutely correct and justified in pushing me to spend time with the kids. It's an easy excuse to blame work for simply being a bad Dad. Thank God she pushed as she did. As it was, I wasn't the best Dad, but I would have been far, far worse had Vangie not coached in the background.

Thing at EP also had a big change for us. I started working for a new boss recently hired by Keith Price. His name was Bob York. He was an engineer who relocated to America from England.

Bob was an ex-rugby player who carried ample physical scars from years of playing a contact sport with no protective equipment. His nose had been broken countless times and was spread on his face like a melted piece of candy on a hot summer's sidewalk. He had cauliflower ears from the years of pummeling by aggressive, testosterone-filled, professional rugby wannabes. He was now quite stocky from years of inactivity that relocated most of his muscles to the belly region. However, he seemed to be a good old bloke. Pardon the poor attempt at colloquialism.

Bob was a decent sort of guy, and I liked hearing him speak in his Cockney accent. He taught me how to properly pronounce 'aluminum.' According to him, it was pronounced owl-looo-minni-umm. When he was wound up or drinking (which usually coincided), he became difficult to understand due to not restraining his strong accent.

Bob carried with him a heavy attitude of superiority. By his recollection, the utility industry in jolly old England was much further advanced than in the United States or elsewhere in the known universe. Despite all these things,, he was a very sharp travel partner. Lucky for all of us, he didn't write like he spoke.

Bob and his wife had Vangie and I over for dinner at their house one evening. Bob was probably 15 or so years older than us, and dinner degraded quickly to intense work discussions. I was informed after we got back home that night that the evening was, at best, awkward for the wives.

Bob and I worked together very well at EP. Little did I know that we would be thrust together again in future circumstances that were far less pleasant. Regardless, I enjoyed working with Bob at Engineering Physics.

One of the many business-related trips I took for EP was to Orlando Public Utilities in Orlando, Florida. I talked Bob York into allowing us to drive there instead of flying. Paying me mileage for my personal car cost them about the same as the airplane ticket had I flown there, and I was able to take Vangie and the kids.

I took vacation time right after finishing at the Stanton Energy Center in Orlando, and we spent three days at Disney World and Epcot Center. It was enjoyable and entertaining to watch the kids become overwhelmed with sensory overload at Disney World and Epcot.

Oddly, the most memorable moment of the trip was not experienced in the theme parks. It was at a breakfast diner outside the park the morning before visiting Epcot. Vangie, Josh, Brandi, Brittanie, and I were sitting at the table preparing to eat a nice, hot breakfast. This needed to be a good meal due to the highly anticipated mass consumption of junk food while in the park(s).

The kids, overall, were very well-behaved but this morning was problematic. Josh immediately started throwing a fit at the breakfast table as only a two-year-old can do. Vangie was always an amazing mother and usually knew what to do and when to do it. This morning was no exception.

After several unsuccessful attempts to calm him down and regain order at the table, Vangie promptly picked him up and marched outside of the restaurant to apply some parental authority to his backside. As she carried him out for the inevitable disciplinary action, he repeatedly screamed, "NO MAMA, NO!!!"

All eyes in this bustling, chaotic, and completely packed-tight restaurant *IMMEDIATELY* fixated on Mother and wayward Son as the restaurant went silent. This included Brandi, Brittanie, and me.

They weaved between and through the multitude of patrons standing in line to get a table and then out of the glass entrance doors into a packed parking lot. They gingerly sat down on a guardrail that was centered right in front of one of the huge windows looking into the diner. She effectively gave

80% of the diner patrons a front-row seat to the coming *'show.'*

With as much motherly love as any woman could ever display, she explained to him why they were outside and then promptly paddled his little butt.

In fairness to the situation, she gave him two quick swats. A collective gasp immediately sucked all the breathable oxygen from the now-silent diner. She then sat and hugged him tightly, his head on her shoulder until he quit crying. It took a few minutes before the previous din and chaos finally returned to the restaurant. After Josh conceded defeat and stopped crying, they calmly returned to the diner to enjoy a completely cold breakfast.

People who quickly scream "child abuse" do not understand that children must have firm but gentle discipline. *You cannot negotiate with a two-year-old.* What took place in that restaurant was a test of wills. Had Joshua 'won,' a precedent would have been established. A two-year-old child would have learned that throwing a fit always ended with him getting his way.

That morning, Joshua established that throwing a fit in a restaurant had a singular outcome. He learned early on that the dinner table was designed to sit, eat, and not throw a fit. *All three of our kids were delight's to dine with at restaurants when they were young.* This was a good thing because, over the years we ate in a lot of restaurants. Vangie was an amazing, loving mother.

Engineering Physics introduced me to the world of software simulation. It turned out to be a Godsend because many years later, Vangie and I would develop and own a multi-national simulation company. The seed of this was planted during our time in Engineering Physics.

I became deeply involved with simulation EP. I loved it. It didn't take long before I knew I wanted to be involved with simulation forever. It was like running a real plant, but there were no consequences for mistakes. Plus, if the simulator was properly engineered, it would emulate the real plant in every way.

This allowed the user to *experience* plant operation as if they were actually operating the plant. People learn experientially far better than any other method. I was captivated by power plant simulation, and it would last a lifetime.

I became involved with many different simulation projects associated with large power plants of the day. One of them required me to spend time in West Long Branch, New Jersey at a simulation company as a test engineer. I was there intermittently for several weeks. I was able to bring Vangie and the kids up to New Jersey for a few days on one of my visits there.

The first evening we were together, I wanted to take Vangie to a good Italian restaurant. She liked Italian food, and I knew the area had a high population of Italians and Italian restaurants. *I should have pre-screened our restaurant that night.*

I picked what looked like an extremely authentic Italian eatery to dazzle her and the kids with "real" Italian food. It was definitely and unquestionably a "real" Italian restaurant. The menus were in Italian. The waitress spoke very little English, and we were clueless about what to order.

Vangie ordered what she thought was lasagna, and the kids ordered spaghetti. Trying to make this an authentic experience for the kids and Vangie, I asked what the "special" was that night. I don't think the waitress understood what I was asking. I am not sure I knew what I was asking.

She pointed to the most expensive dish on the menu. I knew what calamari was, and it definitely had calamari within its long name. I pointed at this dish and shook my head an approving yes.

The waitress, in broken English, said, *"Are you sure?"*

It is always best to ask a few questions when a question of this nature is posed in a restaurant. I learned my lesson and never made this mistake again. When a waiter or waitress asks, "are you sure?" *Ask some questions.*

After a bit, the waitress brought the kids spaghetti and Vangie's lasagna. At about the same time, we began smelling an unpleasant aroma from the kitchen. It smelled like something dead. It was an incredibly unpleasant aroma that I would call more of an odor than an aroma. As soon as she delivered Vangie's lasagna, she went back to get my dinner. There was a ceiling fan slowly spinning over our table. It provided ample unpleasant wafts of the aroma or odor we had begun smelling a few moments prior.

Out comes our waitress with a large, silver platter. It was accompanied by the highly unpleasant odor we were smelling from the kitchen. On the platter was a large, whole squid on a bed of noodles with what looked like 15 or 20 of her little babies on the perimeter turned upside down to look like flower pedals. The noodles were covered in a red sauce. Unfortunately, the red sauce resembled blood. It seemed they

53

were serving me Mama squid and her sacrificed children. The smell was even less pleasant than the perceived massacre on the platter.

Brittanie immediately began crying while Brandi squealed, "Oooooh, that looks awful. You can't eat that, Daddy." She then began to cry also.

Vangie was gagging from the smell and, jumping up, pulled little Joshua from his high chair and quickly told the girls, "Follow me, *NOW*." They ran out of the restaurant. *Hmmmm… So much for a nice Italian dinner.*

There was nothing embarrassing about sitting at the table with every eye in the restaurant staring at me in silent anticipation of what I would do next. *Okay, truth be known, it was mortifying.* I waved to the waitress. It took her a few minutes, but when she arrived at the table, she had the check in her hand and a bit of a smirk on her face. I gave her my credit card and followed her to the cash register. ***Thirty minutes later, we had a pleasant and happy dinner at McDonalds.***

We also experienced our first hurricane. Yes, in Maryland, of all places. Hurricane Gloria hit Maryland in September of 1985. We were warned, ad-nauseum, of its potential seriousness as it progressed northward. The much-anticipated event was windy and rained harder than we had ever seen rain come down, but for us, it was largely anti-climactic.

We were shopping at the beautiful Columbia Mall the very next day. Other than a few tree limbs on the street, damage was minimal in Columbia. Sadly, Long Island and other northward venues were not near as lucky. They attributed 8 deaths to the storm.

Unfortunately or fortunately (???), we could not escape the call of the West. We missed the wide-open spaces and wanted to be nearer to family. The larger issue was; my unrelenting travel schedule. It was taking its toll on us as a family. Once again, we began looking for plants that were hiring operators and supervisors. One of these plants was Deseret G&T's Bonanza Plant, located outside Vernal, Utah.

Bonanza was supposed to be a two-unit plant, but Deseret G&T (the owner) built just one 450 MW coal fired plant as they determined the second one was not needed.

I would have never believed it had someone told me we were going back to Utah again... I just wouldn't have believed it. Oddly, it was about to happen, and once again, *our lives were changed forever...*

www.ingramcontent.com/pod-product-compliance
Lightning Source LLC
Chambersburg PA
CBHW070944120626
46546CB00004B/1552